by Tom Clark

Airplanes (1966)
The Sandburg (1966)
Emperor of the Animals (1967)
Stones (1969)
Air (1970)
Neil Young (1971)
The No Book (1971)
Green (1971)
Smack (1972)
John's Heart (1972)
Blue (1974)
At Malibu (1975)
Fan Poems (1976)
Baseball (1976)
Champagne and Baloney (1976)
35 (1976)
No Big Deal (1977)
How I Broke In (1977)
The Mutabilitie of the Englishe Lyrick (1978)
When Things Get Tough on Easy Street: Selected Poems
     1963–1978 (1978)
The World of Damon Runyon (1978)
One Last Round for The Shuffler (1979)
The Master (1979)
Who Is Sylvia? (1979)
The Great Naropa Poetry Wars (1980)
The Last Gas Station and Other Stories (1980)
The End of the Line (1980)
A Short Guide to the High Plains (1981)
Heartbreak Hotel (1981)
The Rodent Who Came To Dinner (1981)
Journey to the Ulterior (1981)
Nine Songs (1981)
Under the Fortune Palms (1982)
Dark As Day (1983)
Jack Kerouac (1984)
Paradise Resisted: Selected Poems 1978–1984 (1984)
Property (1984)
The Border (1985)
Late Returns: A Memoir of Ted Berrigan (1985)
His Supposition (1986)
Kerouac's Last Word (1986)
The Exile of Céline (1987)
Disordered Ideas (1987)
Apocalyptic Talkshow (1987)
Easter Sunday (1988)
Jack Kerouac in San Francisco (1989)
The Poetry Beat: Reviewing the Eighties (1990)
Fractured Karma (1990)

TOM CLARK

FRACTURED KARMA

BLACK SPARROW PRESS
SANTA ROSA   1990

Cover painting by John Register.
Waiting Room for the Beyond, 1983.
Oil on canvas. 50 x 55 inches.

ACKNOWLEDGEMENTS

Some of the poems in this book first appeared in the following magazines: *Antaeus, Before Columbus Review, Blind Date, City Lights Review, Exquisite Corpse, Giants Play Well in the Drizzle, Harvard Magazine, Intent, In This Corner, New American Writing, Peninsula, Santa Monica Review, St. Mark's Poetry Project Newsletter, Taos Review, Temblor, This Is Important, Witness* and *ZYZZYVA*.

"For Robert Duncan" appeared in *The Best American Poetry, 1989* (Macmillan/Collier).

Black Sparrow Press books are printed on acid-free paper.

LIBRARY OF CONGRESS CATALOGING-IN-PUBLICATION DATA

Clark, Tom, 1941–
  Fractured karma / Tom Clark.
    p.   cm.
  ISBN 0-87685-792-6 : — ISBN 0-87685-791-8 (pbk.) :
    — ISBN 0-87685-793-4 (signed) :
  I. Title.
PS3553.L29F7   1990
811'.54—dc20   90-30676
                                                               CIP

Table of Contents

Fractured Karma

PRELUDE: WAITING ROOM FOR THE BEYOND

*When I see an empty chair I
often think that someone has
died. Pursuing that suggestion
it is not all that big a step
to put clouds out the window
as though one is miles in the air.*

—John Register

1.

Death greets life in a moment of liftoff.
In this moment one may read divine intent,
Less ominous than luminous, less fade than loft:
A plum light, Mars violet, blent
By angled sunlight in an expansive flooding.
The empty room floats miles off the ground.
Out the window piled violet cumulus
Softly masses as if viewed by some half
Dozing flier alerted in turbulence to glance
Out over the roof of heaven toward a fleeing
Grainy horizon built with layered drifts
Of air diffusely vanishing into forever:
Before this window full of light which sifts
Life itself away, we see a chair, empty.

2.

Some space traveler who has drifted off
Into death or momentary reverie is now invited
To return, through blue avenues of ozone,
To this room where reflected and direct
Sunlight have fused, as a daydream comes
To seem like some imagined hereafter smoothly
Blank, atonal and natural.
A beckoning is sounded with clarity pure
And cool, the deeper space adds a
Previously absent vastness to the view.

3.

The reflected square of sunlight
On the floor before the waiting
Empty chair is an unpremeditated
Cerulean blue. The bluish white
Sunlight that butters the sill spreading
Its radiance out to spill over edges
Of deep violet shadows welling
Up beneath broad windows is rich
And shaded, a sugarlike nutrient
That sustains attention beyond nostalgia
And expectation. All life is a process
Of removal from life.

4.

Sunlight spills like plasm from a beaker
Across the glassy floor at long
Severe winter afternoon angles.
The empty chair waits squarely facing
The dazzled planetary viewer
For whom this scene of chilly serenity
Has been composed as if by a detached
Creator on his way out of his floating
World. You move forward feeling
Yourself falling under this spell that is
Hardly anything at all, nameless,
Yet who escapes it?

5.

Hidden in the quiet skybound gray
Aerie of the dove violet blue-plum silky
Original flooding generation light
Of creation, hidden or else absent, no
World extends outside this space-washed room, no
Sensation beyond the time-washed somatic moment.

6.

Miles above the life of the
Distant city the sunlight
Filters through and washes with oxygen
The pure rich blood that spills
Color out through the glass:
Sleep without dreams. The night's soul
Cleaning over, refreshed, the first
Step I take will lead directly
To the second, the clouds will pile
Up soft as carpeting beneath
My feet, I will return through
The flood of sunlight and take
My seat.

1. The Possessed Winter Dusk

Arctic Cold Snap

The cherry ball on the mercury stick drops off at three zero
Off to the left the iridescent glow of the sea glances
Gold and hard in the thin indifferent sun
Ah and all the green and growing things wonder what hit them

Nasturtium hibiscus and clover shriveling
Noiseless as fear on a wide wilderness
This heavy blast from the polar freezer fuses
Leaf arteries into obelisks of bright glass

Quivering in the coldwave's intenser day the Mind
Republic meanwhile narrows and darkens likewise
Host to dim shades as the moon compels them on
Driven space ghosts before an enchanter fleeing

The long weight of light's pain scored infinity
Keeps sleep from ever easing our agitated songs
Still tall redwoods charmed by high volt stars
Dream and so dream on all day with no stir

As in the selfsame beat of time's broad wingspan
A thin jet roars by among the bleak grown pines
Like a light blot of gray water color bleeding
Spreading the deep possessed winter dusk across country

Blues for Eric Dolphy

As traffic slowly hones the blade of evening
Throbbing unchained in the plum dark afternoon
We take courage to seek oracles of older gods
Who sow the revenge of things in the river of cars
Flooding from here to Golden Gate Fields of Eternity
Like a thin wash of gray water color bleeding

Dear worlds we've never known nor ever will
Traffic in bondage to ambition holds hearts in thrall
Anxious dreams sift through these shifting headbeams
Scattering eyes of light across dusk's drift and growth
With a flash of pulses like a suicidal star
Matchflares detaching night tides from dayshore

Through winter's glowing exact cold machinery
We are howling or beating out our souls once more
While above East Bay's heavy green shoulders
Soprano sax floats seaward over automotive rapids
Angels of the jetstream sighing lip service to creation
Amid the galactic junkdrift toward Arcturus

Whippoorwill Beckoning In Winter

Whippoorwill beckoning in winter from nowhere's glade
By first stars' shoreward tether to this darkling gulf
Release your unchained streaming nightshade lanterns
Looking out upon the white race tracks toward Arcturus
To handicap the pain of several animal eternities

Dear worlds I've never known nor ever will
I hear your soprano sax sounds floating seaward
And in them an angel on one shoulder sighing
Like a diamond or a cry to guide and reconcile
The time wandering inmate to this bone asylum

Through winter twilight's glowing exact cold
A thin wash of gray water color is bleeding
As traffic slowly hones the blade of evening
And scatters its eyes across dusk's drift and growth
Muffled lamps lighting up only the bearers

The Hour Illumination Blockers Slide Away

Black clouds mass over East Bay hills
As traffic slowly hones the blade of evening
To carve sketches of Spain up to the hilt
And scatter its rice across dusk's drifting canyon

From the left the iridescent glow of the sea glancing
The winter twilight growing exact and cold
Lays its high resolution display across all our terminals
And we are howling or beating out our souls

In disturbed syllables before the brightly lit dot pattern
Emitted by Tokyo into Jerusalem foiled sky
While through the tall redwood the wild wind draws its scythe
With a flash of fans like a suicidal diva

Who lies down on the floor and pretends to be dead
Due to a clanging without relief under the skull roof
As traffic slowly grinds the knife of twilight
Like a false diamond or a cry of groundless hope

The Possessed Winter Dusk

Soprano sax sound floating seaward
Over East Bay hills' heavy green shoulders
Drawn by the dark earth rising plants
I hold on to the night's dark mane
In the hollow bowl of the drum of the body
Like some buffalo soldier on an Indian pony

Attention

Dawn's faded apparitions of the undead just stealing
Back into the trunks of cypress still at overnight
Minimum fahrenheit I ventured
Into that strange eternity gossamer-fall

A swarm of sparkling particles down-drifting
Iridescent snowbugs parachuting? A slow
Solar drizzle into the kneehigh mist layer
That was forming above the tall grass?

In the great vault overhead however
Was emerging cloudlessly the color blue
Coming into being on an unstained
Cadet's blouse of ozone, ruling out rain or snow

A grasper after manna with palms outflung
I discovered this microflorescent flutter
Of atoms in reverse liftoff away from heaven
Was actually minute ice spicules

Out of which arose a rainbow fragile
As water colors thinly brushed on kleenex
Or the difference between breathing
And practically everything else

Ocular Oracles

Of those who haunt the
higher air dimensions   imaginal fields

in the long surrenderings of space   I sing
those faces like notes that swim

up through the glass of time   translucent
as gin in crystal   ghost eyes

of lunar sprites and other   almost seen
things   On the inky edges of this

diastasis   they appear
to collect the color that drains

out of skin in moonlight
as night comes on   they accumulate

phantom shapes   making
dusk kindle with a

million thoughts of nothing

Solstice

Cold floating days, difficult to keep body
Temp. up as planet cools off mysteriously
This P.M. two small grey birds bumped
Around in the rose bush for a while
A capella (no rush hour for once)
In last rays of tinny Christmas sun
While voluntary trumpets were quietly
Emitted by radio into Jerusalem foiled sky
Far off and to our great astonishment
O blue earth sounds your golden flower
From the bell of its silver horn
I didn't think it would ever come back on

Presence

Thinking at wild day's blowing advent of creation and rebirth as
    the magicians' natural presence in the world
Magi forever power gliding on divine tailwinds to discover the
    mystery proposed in Babylonian hieroglyphs
(Enameled eyes searching out the god in green wet hay piled up
    on a rough bed of dry redwood needles)
I rode out this selfsame solstitial tempest pursuing the zero
    protected from the storm by the sidereal numbers
(Optical calculus of the hyper real over oxygenated Navajo
    campfire stars)
I tried to send through these quest sentences of my own to a time
    wandering missel thrush I noticed soldiering into the wind
An upstream swimmer being blown back through the breezy
    avenue of trees beneath which Prospero's
Enchanted menagerie lay parked among the other curiously
    willing animal sculptures
(When does the limy door become detached to free the temporary
    occupant, What exact temperature decides
The hour illumination blockers slide away releasing the dream
    parachutist back into the slipstream?)
But as my inventory of queries grew I didn't notice the too short
    blue day was rapidly disappearing
While I paused failing to coax that struggling bird to stop and
    bathe at the imagination wash
A fool moon splashed in full enormity across the swaying boughs
    heavy laden with many colored nativity lights

2. Fractured Karma

Under the Sign of Thoth

Early morning light archery on the Nile
Feather forming as space curves away
We are chanting the book of the dead in blue & green
Two gospel hummingbirds gleaming in the rain

Space starts to tremble because it wants to go places
The galleys' chant unchains a foam of sound
As heavenward the Pharaoh tilts his prow
Over river silences where all thought glides

After making love to the river all night long
Psyche asks why love's so dark in Egypt
Moved by a slow blunt impulse as if snowblind
She is still waiting on the moon palace stairs

Sighing with sensitive quince and mauve explosions
As if she understood the wind & the rain
The soft wince when the marvelous sweet fruit turns out bitter
Men are like that she says

Cassandra

A primordial age underlies all events now
Moved by some blunt impulse as if snowblind
This is the hour when the mysteries emerge
Drawn by the dark earth rising plants
She expressed herself in many different ways
Saying "I've lost control again"
The fatality the girl from Kentucky

Everything is determined from before
Fate has dragged Snow White away
With a flash of pulses like a suicidal star
And we are howling or beating out our souls
Somehow it all makes sense though not really
There is none of that sharp outline we think of as reality
And she is still waiting on the moon palace stairs
As if she understood the wind & the rain

Fractured Karma

Early morning light archery off a far boom shore
Thrust bellies to the air fool moon's plum shades awaken
Beneath them voice & ghost curve away to ocean deeps
In the hollow bowl of the drum of the body

Moon pictures propped on the morning gestalt
A plum gray flood of light Pollock would have killed for
Its full Rig Veda morning alarm glow rising
Like water bubbles into a drowner's mouth

Psyche's Clear Lake Riverhood Shining Looking Glass Cold

Psyche asks why love's so dark
She is plucking a sweet olive branch from the moon palace
As if she understood the wind & the rain
In the hollow bowl of the drum of the body

She is still waiting on the moon palace stairs
After making love to the river
With a flash of scales like a suicidal fish
Amid the galactic junkdrift toward Arcturus

Eternity Time Share Rebus

He is reclining like a river god on a rock
She is plucking a sweet olive branch from the moon palace
There is none of that sharp outline we think of as reality
A breeze drives wisps of fog across the pale moon
Like a thin wash of gray water color bleeding
Down into the flat topped fortune telling plane trees
The joyous body chemistry bubble balloon of youth
Breaks and we free fall through the leaves
And when we land he is still reclining like a river god
And she is still waiting on the moon palace stairs

Pharaoh's Blues

Psyche you are able to read across Time's face
From right to left the Chinese conception of fate
Moves across the sky on a warm gulf cloud
There where no language ever yet was known
Your clear lake riverhood shining looking glass cold
Generates metabiology at the delta junction
Between the large cosmos and this microzone around your hips
Where memory guides me to perform in imagination
What is after nature's untuning no longer the expected song
Yet despite the ceaseless sapphire tears of my collapse
Let one thing be understood I'm not dead completely
To these panic signals you emit via thought charged sky
I'm just back here under the mind palms regrouping
And putting a few last finishing touches on my booty boats
Before the ceremonies of the divine cargo cult take over

Seduction In the Wider Fields of Eternity

Where the gulf sky is separated from the gulf by a thin blue line
In the hollow bowl her body made when intersected by mine

Psyche's clear lake riverhood shining looking glass cold
Mirrored my life back up to me from the depths of that hollow
 bowl

By biological predetermination the ancient Egyptian
Word for kiss was derived from the verb to eat

A memory that vibrates long after the string is plucked
Creating a note sustained by the reverberating of her body

To fill to capacity the consciousness of the chosen one
So there is no escaping the ever rekindled hunger

To Psyche

Everything happens to you if you know it
I turn to the redwing moon for control
Its small cornstalk fringes slide apart
Opposite ways over bone thought oceans
While the stars come out Confucius blue
Above your small hair smooth knob belly
The ghost of a change happens to you
Even if I don't know it yet

To Psyche As Time's End Nears

O goddess give this untuned song strung
Together out of hard wire and short memory
A listen and forgive me for singing
Your own sweet soft excuses back into your ear
The wild wave sound deserting the conch
And going back into the ocean always
Behaves that way or am I dreaming like the planet
Since daylight over us now possesses no more power

Than the furnace of Nebuchadnezar over the three
Companions of Daniel of whom not one
Hair on their heads was so much as singed
Shadrack Meshack and Abednego
Of those three also do you enable me to sing
And every other thing and all of this too
Must be forced back into the creation seashell
Before you and I are to do any more sleeping

Perishable Memo

I saw your body swim up the vivid night sky
A silvery white weight wet haired
Salmon breasting fire tides in silk swift ascension
While on the wide flowing black periphery
Wild stars flared out and showered
Failing to follow you in your higher leaping motion

But with my memory that fluid shape too will die
No one will see what I've seen
No one will go where I've been
Wan worlds from which the colors drained away
Leaving only these strange unearthly word outlines

3. Blind Flight

Inauguration Day

Brings no change save frown lines forming in the turning moon's
    faces
O my Imagination in whom I've placed all hope
I croon to you from the cliff edge over which your strange logic
Fatally pulls me on toward dangerous smiling breakers

Still O Total Buddha your swift ability to slice through
The green seaweed that silently preempts thinking
Is a deeper keel that continues to cut dream smoothly
Across a cool enduring sibilance of wind rain & sun

Even when in mind swirling nights of planet eclipse
The blind hummingbird moon disappears deviously
Through the slit in your palmwing mindshade
Around the mothglow afterimage nevertheless hangs on

A broken arc to ransom dawn
As we gaze upon the world without you for the first time

Blind Flight

The white distances beyond the Golden Gate spawn fifth
Dimension field shelters from the vast incremental and remaining
Throwweight of pain left over after the many
Years of tears & lying kicked up by the first four
Space time depth and that other the strange ungainly
Loss of soul control coordinates I originally noticed in dreams
About six months ago when I first found myself
Blind flying through these dark ion haze days

Aqualung

Slow cling of gray white rain at oyster dawn
As if thin cloth were being continually torn
Inside outside, soft sizzle of wet rubber
Hugging four lanes of blacktop traffic back
Firing bridgeward over this slicing sluiceway
That cuts slick and gleaming as a blade
Through dull wool light leaking from blue pleura

Caught

So this is it: washed up on my island
My hands sweat and uncalm silence
Cancels sleep with echoes of abjection
And confused winds rustling slack sails

The continuous swirlings-up of life
That precede death the way sex precedes anxiety
Or anger leads to sorrow suggest a flat
Faced dimensionless timepiece

A particulate universe that has no space
And which once tinkered with opens out
Into the cosmos like a fan without hinges
One evening in antiquity the sun slides down

The emotional vibrato that bends long
Vowels like strings tensed too tight:
Tomorrow never knows the difference, though
That won't get you off the hook of tonight

The Night of the Nonconsumer

Dumbed out, jacked around, used, bought, stiffed
(To freelance for earthlings is to leave humanity behind)
I jockey my bike all night across town to close
In on that infinite cartoon slow lane beyond
Thought of work, in which tires grab no asphalt, cease

To turn, releasing the spinning cyclist
Out of the system into the night, the night of
The nonconsumer adrift amid vacant
Dreaming malls and marts of a turning world
Of space which is only selfconsuming

There no business is done, no lies are told
The stars seem close, but on those heavenly bodies
One has no purchase to negotiate
Their heat will not burn me down, by their lights
I will return at last to my own planet

Quasimodo

Inside the big clock things get strange
Noisily you seek a motive for feeling
Find silence waiting in your life script
Where another fate's mirrored for you
In time's revelation it's a pain
Like death to see beauty gaining
And only your fading memorials
Of some words to show for it

A Strange New Religion

Down beneath the blue region there's an under hum
Which indicates the issue between us is no longer forgiveness
But understanding of the long numbness of the night
And patience and courage to ignore dumb thoughts
About death and life until at last dawn comes
Once again with its implications of the routine
Ways of knowing and acquiring and accepting by which
Unbelievably we are once more allowed to forget all this
And the last temptation of Christ appears in a new light

Detachment

Dream from which I wake owning a glass heart
Whoever owns nothing drifts outside life more easily

A porous sky of light cheesecloth
Muffles the black diamond of the mind

Detaching the diver from the sky
While the light falls by soundlessly

Nehru's Nation

Dreams confuse and deceive
more and more with the years. One night
the Grim Reaper in hooded caftan
cracking his knuckles and coughing out
through Khomeini whiskers the grave
choked vowels of Islam teaches
a sunken basement acting class
in Hollywood. While kid tv stars
chant memorized verses from
the Koran Grim glares at me
declaring in throat rattling Arabic
I must write a poem called "Nehru's
Nation" though when I wake up
I can't be sure it wasn't really
"Nehru's Notion" which makes no sense.
I worry about it, become more
impossible than usual to live with
then one night find myself traveling
through this tall dream wheatfield
in the shade of these low dark trees.
The white wheat waves in one windy
flat top unison lean like
that flat blowing grass you see
in certain Hopper paintings where
the people in the picture seem to know
Fate has dragged Snow White away
under those low dark trees, soon
to emerge in blood stained overalls
for fresh victims. Out of that dream
wheatfield now steps a man
in an aviator's cap with long
blue earflaps tumbling down
to his shoulders, a sanskrit
insignia at the crown. As I look on
the wind begins to ravel up
his earflaps, wrapping them around
his head into a turban. The tall
wild wheat waves into the
low dark Nebraska Sweden death trees.

I recognize this is his beautiful
sweet death nation. He beckons
in a gesture of invitation but dreams
confuse and deceive
so that as I move to follow the wind waves
sieve through me, failing to carry me along.

Subject

distrusts all pasts
conditionals and perfects
future continuous too

suffers
fallibility of memory, senses that
history is compound
of minute particles, questions
whether event exists
if unrecorded, hears noise

of one small plane
passing over rather high up
gradually diminishing into nothing,
                              cool,

lightweight, ancient
as Buddhist conception of fate
in successive incarnations,

then hears the big
ships begin to hum

Patriarchy Dream

I go to investigate a gathering of the future kings.
A man in Levis talks at length about how
a primordial age underlies all events now,
Everything is predetermined from before.
A hero, he says, frees his ego with the help of
women, on whose knees the future kings recline
        when they wish for rest.

The fluid dividing line between
        two gospel hummingbirds
throbbing a yard above the dart azalea
gives me a chance to see (later)
all the doors and windows closed
in on themselves on the last day
in a final dazed ruse of the creator,
the begetter and supremo of the whole
        world operation.

Karma

Karma simply means that you don't
let your left hand know what your right
hand is doing, getting through to
tomorrow (also known as existence)
simply means that your left
hand wouldn't want to know anyway

Signs & Omens

When Calchas the bird interpreter started to talk
Wind-running Achilles sat down and said "Seer
Tell us anything you may have learnt from heaven
Take courage and speak the oracles of the gods
Here by the hollow ships nobody will hurt you"

But then Lord Agamemnon jumped up furious
His eyes hard little points bespeaking a black
Passion still filling his heart over past oracles
"Nobody can know everything" he said
"Not even the best of diviners" and as he spoke
Sentries inched forward into dark daylight

Memo to prophets: Soothsay all the strange
Things you want to soothsay but keep in mind
Unless you have friends in very high places
Ten minutes of blameless divining
Can get you ten years behind a heavy oar deep
In the hold of some swift black cargo ship

Job Listing

A person who drinks his or her own
urine and stomps around in the moonlight
howling and playing watchee watchee.

A solitary medium.

No training necessary. Apply within.

Angry Descent of Apollo

I

Dreadlock sky-elder clouds bend low over November
Dogs barking outside stone gates in winter twilight
A clanging without relief under the skull roof takes
Over this silent white king space of the Greeks

As a bronze bow was once held tense over
The earth and with a clang night fell in
One sweep of the god's drawn back arm
Sounding a single resonant note like the close of a Bach Partita

II

Although they were made strong by this story some god had
    given it to them
Who did not give it to us so we must stand back by the hollow
    boats
When we turn around we will immediately recognize
The goddess for her two eyes gleam terribly

As jewel fluorocarbon nicks in the World Seam shot through
By the god they call the Peashooter or Trigger Happy One
Whose sport firing tricks apart her plentiful nets and helixes
And this is why a death curse has befallen these people

In the form of a contagion that breaks loose initially among their
    animals
As the first angry metal arrows aimed at the feet of the fleeing
    dogs move faster
Than the silvery flash produced as an errant phosphene
Flutters across the eye of night falling over the lakes of Central
    Africa

And now the pyres blaze day and night and though
The terrible roar of the sea is still pleasing to the goddess
When the thinned out ranks of the people go down to the sea
    now to sing
The noise is no longer pleasing to the goddess in her soul

A Night Voyage

There broke into the deep sleep in my head
Heavy waves of thunder of thunder and I jumped
Like somebody awakened by force

There was a lot of rubble a lot of rubble on the sidewalks
Parts of buildings parts of buildings had come down
There were decorative fixtures lying in the street and on the
    sidewalk
The sprinkler system of one building had gone off
It was creating a waterfall down one of the walls
People talked about how pretty how pretty it was

There was a continuous sighing that rose up into the air
A sighing that rose into the black air and created a trembling
A continuous trembling that shook that shook the black air

And then we came out of that place of the trembling air
And we ventured out upon the ruined bridge
And came at length to the point where the last stone was broken
    off
The breath was spent from my lungs and I could go no further

And then we felt a movement as when a thick fog breathes
Or when night darkens over darkens over our hemisphere
And in the distance there appears a mill which the wind turns

When we got to the Ferry Building we saw a huge crowd waiting
    on a pier
Everybody just standing in line in the dark and scared now really
    scared

We moved away from San Francisco which was totally dark
And went under the blacked out bridge and the dark city moved
    away
It was like being in the Sierras you could see so many stars

4. Tree Talk

The Fall of Birds

To drink the sun's energy like a plant
Yet to distinguish neither violet nor blue
The two colors of your flight environment
The needlelike waverings of your compass trued
On a black light at planet central
Tend toward pure white
This is the aerial state which defines you before language

And yet a need remains to speak of gravity
You dream in the same night in which I am towed down
And though buoyed by a steady space euphoria
Of which I will never have the slightest knowledge
You too will grow weary with the blood surge
And become the plummet of your own weight
To be printed as a particulate sign
Upon the blank page of earth history

Losing your meaning as words do
Just prior to the dissolution into feeling

Tree Talk

Tree talk is the party line of the intelligent listening forest
Whether the smooth voiceless no breeze whisper rustling
Inside green upper tiers of a fogbound blue spruce
Or the deep aether growth song stirring way
Down in each tender quiet working sub-earth redwood shoot

Nervous Tree Talk

W-waves roll out of big trees @ 3 ft./sec. accelerating in air 5 x
    and gaining
Directionality upon log truck's initial grinding uphill gear box
    rumble

During the ensuing wild fear spasm preluding full metal entry
These waves modulate into general non electrical soul emergency
    alarms
By which the great dense thronged atmosphere transformers
    notify and alert one another
With anxious emanations slower yet more intense than light
    beams
Heralding the loud saw blade's first quickening shiver through the
    grove

At the Pain Factory Site: Construction Phase (New Gods)

First the perverted concept then the actual mind capture
Into the waking trees amid the dreams which fall uneasy
Come the chainsaw destroyers of worlds sent by Doctor Science
With their earth rumbling dumptrucks & sky puncturing cranes
And following them in ever ascending rank of wizardry
First the architects & lawyers armed with punch lists & battle
    plans
Then the dedicated technicians of civilized animal torture
In neat smock coats with blood & money on their white hands

And so the Western Blue Cedar shall drift no more
Over these hillsides like a mountain river sighing
Nor shall tall Manna Gum or Canary Island Pine
Climb through purple morning fogs to drink
From the wild flowing jetstream & become strong
In the construction phase at the Animal Research Facility
Beyond the long blue & gold storm fences
Now one can hear the violent tossing together of new gods

On this site you of the impossible future may find some sign
Amid seared girders & broken concrete reading "Here
Where humans once strolled pleasant shaded pathways
Through groves of their own thoughtful plantation & design
A different breed of being later passed through & left behind
Not merely the unremembered cries of beasts in agony
Nor their flashburn mutations & strange atrocity scars

But these ruined deities you see crumbling here before you
These fallen likenesses of Arbitrariness handmaiden of
    Compulsion
And chipped plaster images of Brutalidad god of Power
Whose hard rites dominated among the apemen during these
    times"

At the Northwest Animal Facility, As the Work Continues

> *Ungentle men! They cannot thrive—*
> *To kill thee! Thou ne'er didst alive*
> *Them any harm: alas, nor could*
> *Thy death yet do them any good . . .*
> *It cannot die so. Heaven's King*
> *Keeps register of everything:*
> *And nothing may we use in vain.*
> *E'en beasts must be with justice slain,*
> *Else men are made thy deodands.*
> *Though they should wash their guilty hands*
> *Yet could they not be clean . . .*
>
> —Andrew Marvell

The sad root pines in secret underground
As do surviving sister eucalypti all around
Mourning great ghost trees where they fell
Before the long shadow of Intellectual Evil

Tangled in a hyper real mosaic knot of fear
With the less witting creatures they will torture
The researchers lack even the courage to show their faces
Here on the site of their future killing places

Civilization

The wild weeds that think the
rainy weather's
heaven

—life forms
jump into existence in
one night—

are totally right
(though that thought comes in
the middle of civilization)

Inside the Redwood

Floating tiers and worlds
a green heaven doll house

dense microwood spaces
needle masses stretch out

big rain shroud wings over
air runways imagined solid

as clouds flown through in planes
thick stacked tufted landings

branch bales piled up feathery
no sky shows through

in there the greens so dark
like blacks with orange edged

light lower lift-ups
of needle tip droopers poised

to move up and down in
the water weighted wind

"Needle masses stretch out . . ."

Needle masses stretch out
Big rain shroud wings over
Dense microwood spaces

A green heaven dollhouse
No sky shows through
In the great vault overhead however

Two gospel hummingbirds
Fly by lightweight ancient
As Chinese conception of fate

Marshy Breathing

Toebiters capture air from pond top taking back bubbles in tiny
    wing tanks
Or swimming off encased in silver bubble cloaks
Riffle beetles live on an air blanket caught in micro-body-hairs
Back swimmers ease up to surface on inflated bumper suspenders
Then head down fast thrust bellies to the air
Mosquito wrigglers suck in air through long thin snorkel tubes
Tadpoles surface gulp oxygen like mouth breathing people
Damsel flies flail leaflike tufted ventral air intake gills
Larval aqua bugs are themselves overgrown gills adept at air
    absorption
Dragonfly nymphs like yogis are able to draw in water through
    their natural
Output pipe then push it back out again by air jets
Amphibious plants reach to light for air manna
Submarine bulkhead networks allow floating aquatic greenery
To collect and preserve air in minute pontoons
Interconnected airchambers inside tule stems
And those of cattails & reeds & other bulrushes
Conduct gases on which the entire fertile delta system
Of creation depends as Moses knew

Linnaeus' Flower Clock

6 AM	Spotted Cat's-ear opens
7 AM	African Marigold opens
8 AM	Mouse-ear Hawkweed opens
9 AM	Prickly Sow-thistle closes
10 AM	Nippleworth closes
11 AM	Star of Bethlehem opens
12 NOON	Passion-flower opens
1 PM	Childing Pink closes
2 PM	Scarlet Pimpernel closes
3 PM	Hawkbit closes
4 PM	Small Bindweed closes
5 PM	Water-lily closes
6 PM	Evening Primrose opens

Linnaeus leaned forward on his hands
in a rhapsody of taxonomy
outside the medical faculty hall at Uppsala University
and knew the hour exactly
simply by glancing down at
the frail Moschatel or Town-hall clock
which bears at its stem tip five small flowers
four encompassing its perimeter
like the four faces of a clock
the fifth pointing straight up at
the sky habitation
of a tidy clockmaker god
on whose star circuits this whole vivid time garden was modeled

5. An Obsession

An Obsession

Refused in Lisbon he kept his self belief
Before the Salamanca Committee he quoted the prophet Esdras
To prove the world was smaller than a single thought
A grand landmass he contended lay close beyond the setting sun
The committee of scholars trotted out Aristotle and Augustine
The world was too big and anyway mostly water
Interrupted here and there by impassable bulkheads they said

He loved his own obsession
He kept his self belief
Nine years after his first failed pitch at the Portuguese Court
Isabella Queen of Castile entrusted him with a few small ships
He sailed with little else except the blind confidence of fixation
After planting under the unfortunate palms
The sticks and rags of his employer and her gods
He lightened the locals of a little of their gold
Sold a few of their wild souls into slavery
Then sailed home triumphant he thought

He came back to disgrace and jail
He kept his self belief
Throughout his endless tiltings against the Eastern Dragon
Only he could see its myth quality
Its full Rig Veda morning alarm glow rising
Flaring up lifeward and archaic in the West Indian dawn

When he died
He laid down his head
In a house in Valladolid
Less than a mile from the one
In which Cervantes would be born

Short History of the Americas

Drake dragging back the bloated
booty boats to his faded
evil smelling anglo queen

Vanna White
helping the white hooded Pizarro Bros. spin
the Inquisition wheel

Jump

In the brilliance of the late stages
of the human species
Flying saucer discs emit green laser streams
into digital blue lagoons
Highways rise in the air pitch and dazzle
                    Cities of light spin
at deafening speed full of sound and fury
a 14 foot high hologram emerges from
a diamante Fabergé egg
like Christmas at Neiman Marcus
                    but nothing signifies

The Pure Products of America, Much Later

Banquo's Ghost, this time round, is
the link with everything as
the lonely girl at the broken down
gas station fights
Fate for the man she loves—
and will expose not only her body but her mind
to save the strange runaway
and the drunken brute of a surrogate
father—played by Harry Dean Stanton—
but the real dark interior—
the autistic child of the wilderness—
the fatality—the girl from Kentucky—
history from below—
is played by Kim Basinger—
a trashy thirteen with no past
an angel on one shoulder sighing
and perched smiling on the other a Dark Plan Witch
like a kind of radical Teleology—

Life In Movies

Sharp report
Quick lipstick
Symbols on the mirror
Globes of light spun
In the dark cold night
Fireworks at the shore
Where power roars in
On breakers broken
By a pin into the moon
Travel reveals more
Of life in movies
We who are moved by
Clouds at midnight
Have grasped the illusion
Crossing the black room
A bright beam lights
The thin sheet
With a shadow mark
Some star poses
A presence in scarlet
Carnival laughter
And then the car
Pointed into soft darkness
Starts up like a knife

An Unnoticeable Star (1905–1986)

just another pretty face
but behind that blank
and vapid mask

a supercilious nonchalance
with just a faint
undercurrent of malice

a safecracker hiding his
whiskey bottles in the chandelier
with a subdued flair
for dark emotional stories

both cursed and coolly
exploited his unnatural
gifts
      something disturbing
yet horribly true about
his mixture of extreme
irritation and disbelief
with almost gentlemanly disgust

something about reality
ray milland couldn't stand

To Ungaretti

On high the fables blaze

Giusep', you knew the hard
Egyptian stars
twenty years
before you ever set foot
on the factual shore
of that land whose modern poetry
you were to become
the father of, Italy

And similarly
your I
is grave and slow
and your longing gains
on what it longs for
deliberately
like a quarter horse, strong
but not swift,
taking the thoroughbreds on
at ten furlongs

When I think about you now
I always remember that
under the Southern Cross' wild conflagration
your father
helped build
the Suez Canal

For Robert Duncan

d. February 3, 1988

How the arm moved
throwing the poet's
ashes out of the boat
how it all comes back

How the whole story
form of telling curves
the story around
these cosmic corners

How the stars swam
how the moon
was dying down
out over the water

To loosen out into
those big quiet waters
little pieces of
us all are floating on

For Delmore Schwartz

The night they caught you, I dreamed you sank
Through oozy blooms to lean against a coral tree
Cornered by nebulous cop-fates escaped from ghost tv
On the dime of moonlight where they spidered down
A ladder from the hovering chopper to net you, wan
Beams lighting up a chalky face devoid of color

As some old clown's beginning to make up before a show,
Bright bars still playing about the bone
Like in out-of-focus body scans that give
Too little definition between the known shadow
And the shadow of the actual unknown
From which you always stole away like a fugitive

The Last Words of Hart Crane As He Becomes One
   ## With the Gulf

I have seen my ghost broken my body blessed
And fake Edens built up from my sweat

I admit I wasn't in my right mind
When I quarreled with Peggy and she burned her hand

And took sleeping pills and locked herself in her cabin
And I went down to drown my sorrows among the crewmen

But on that hard morning when the steward knocked upon the
      door
And later I went up on deck in disgrace pyjamas and fresh shiner

The sparkling claret light I thought I saw
While I was folding my coat across the railing

Was actually a reflection of the starry watery floor
With its undersea buddha engines throbbing

1999: A Tale

Prince revolted against his own empire of orgasms
His meadows of soft noise   his warm satin coal
Vanity's stratospheric hair exploded
Chaos rocked the Pulchritude Hotel

Prince rebelled against the human boredom threshold
He ordered blank reality checks soonest
But as time's throttle opened up in stellar overdrive
The tooth of happiness sank wolf deep
The little red corvette spun out
Rubber banshee howling filled the whirlwind road
Prince flailed forward supernormally
Into the blue and pink foam dashboard
Illuminations rolled in an emerald wave
He saw Poinciana branches casting savage hearts
He found black clown light in the moon's charged humming
He spotted thin blue milk bubbles aerating clouds

But even the most beautiful parachutes
Travel away from heaven as they move through the sky

Caravaggio and the Birth of the Baroque Romantic

Though his works hung in the palaces of the King of England the
    Duke of Mantua and several Medici princes he was perhaps
    even better known for his terrible temper and strong taste
    for violent crime
In 1600 he was dragged into court for attacking a man named
    Girolamo Stampa with a club and a sword
In 1601 he wounded a sergeant of arms in a sword fight
Two years later some malicious obscene verses he wrote got him
    sued by a man who would one day become his biographer
In 1604 he flung a plate of artichokes into the face of a tavern
    waiter and once more ended up before a magistrate
That same year police officers twice detained him for yelling "Up
    my ass!" at them in public
In May 1605 he was charged with slandering a woman named
    Laura
Two months later he got into a fight with a law clerk over a
    woman named Lena
After temporary exile he was back in Rome by October at which
    point he again found himself hauled in to court for public
    fighting
The judge fined him 500 scudos and ordered him confined to his
    home
A few weeks later there came a new charge of throwing stones at
    his landlady's window
For months afterwards silence held as Caravaggio's name
    remained absent from the court register
Snow fell on the Spanish Steps melted and was washed away like
    the so-called facts of history
Spring with its earthly glories returned to the Piazza Venezia as
    usual in 1606
On the last day of May the painter got involved in a dispute at
    the tennis court with a man named Ranuccio Tommasoni
    who wound up no longer breathing
In the romantic version this was a rivals' quarrel over the woman
    named Laura
In the movie version Ranuccio was the artist's jealous lover
In the myth version Caravaggio became an outlaw and later
    fatally wounded himself with his own dagger which bore
    the legend "No Hope, No Fear"

In a culminating spasm of intensity he scrawled "I did it" across
    his last canvas in blood
In the painting it appears to be blood spurting from the neck of
    the beheaded St. John
In the history version Caravaggio was merely signing his own
    canvas
In the psychology version he was at last confessing his guilt over
    the murder of Ranuccio
In the art version the signature in blood throbs with subdued
    luminosity like all paint in his hands
Everything seeps away into the chiaroscuro and guiltlessly
    saturates it

Self Portrait: The Artist As Personality

My frenetic overloaded nosedive in Milwaukee provoked hoots
My somber stolid snail's pace at the Toronto Exhibition
Persuaded nobody there was less fun to be had at a cemetery
I performed my lamest most futile repetitive and imitative work
    at Niagara Falls, N.Y.
In front of a giant art-deco cut-out of Beethoven's death mask
And drew horse laughs from the janitors who were the only
    victims left not sleeping
In Rapid City, South Dakota my joyous terminal paeans
    degenerated into a farrago
Exiled to the Northern Peninsula Performance Art Fair
I tossed my hair like a salad until it met my boa flying around
    from the back inducing fission
Chanting through my Laurie Anderson voicebox modulator in my
    best imitation of Spalding Gray
I noticed the critics reacting as though I were dragging chalk
    down a blackboard the wrong way
At the University of Southern Nowhere I drew an audience of one
    dog plus one professor who was doing a thesis on me
Approaching total panic I echoed Blake and slid down the bed-rail
    spreadeagled
In my triumphant comeback bid as Eve singing a very haunting
    Song of Solomon
To Adam in the Garden of Eden on the first morning of the world
And to everyone's surprise it turned out to be the role of my life

Society

Rex Whistler—or is it Joe Isuzu?—stretches
out half naked on a rock and pretends
to be a river god, while Sylvia Plath—or is
that Edith Sitwell down there among the ceramic cherubs?—
lies down on the floor and pretends to be dead.
That's Society. "Reality" is an unmade bed
full of champagne. "I was the first (burp)
to interject my own persona between the lens
and the frilly circus ladies of the human psyche."

A smart model in a Digby Morton suit steps
confidently through the rubble of the Blitz.
That's Society, "her poise unshaken." Hearts
of movie stars and duchesses expand life-jacket style,
Marilyn Monroe's nerves are refused entry to the studio,
and the royal family, from the Super Mum herself
down to Snowdon, Lichfield and Andrew,
parade around cloud cuckoo land in funny hats
while Douglas Fairbanks falls out of filigree windows
and persuades Mountbatten to play Lear in mid air.

Now Mountbatten too is falling falling,
gazing up at their reflections in the mirrored Star Ceiling
Mickey Mouse as the Sheik of Araby
alongside Madame Pompadour as Cassandra
are spinning and flailing, tumbling through space,
berserk boxers doing a minuet in weightlessness,
yet the polystyrene suspension net
slung underneath the scene by Cecil Beaton
somehow makes it all make sense though not really.

Eternal Recurrence

The door to the past is locked, forcing us to guess, so we imagine
the non-success of his long-awaited
marriage night and his subsequent increasing exasperation
as existence shorn of all real difficulty goes on

and on and on. In the autumn of life
though still churning out books
Chesterton tumbles into a slough
of absentmindedness and indulges in much
splashing in his bath requiring the constant
hovering of a housemaid with mop
at the ready. One morning she hears him slosh
out of the tub then a huge splash

of re-entry. "Dammit" the great Catholic storyteller wheezes
through grizzled chops trained to speech in days of
vanished grandeur, Tom Brown and the glorious
Victoria, "I've been here before!"

After Thomas Hardy

Here is the ancient floor
On which the floorboards seem dim
Here was the former door
Through which my dead feet walked in

Here she sits in her chair
Smiling into the fire
Whose light plays about her hair
Like a soldering wire

Though now she has disappeared
Something which still remains
Is surrounded by a glowing beard
Spun from my petrified brains

An Extended Sentence (Jean Genet)

Did the silent 10-year-old standing in the kitchen believe he was
	alone as he stared at the money in the half open drawer?
Did he stretch out his hand?
Was traffic going by in the dark street world below the windows?
Had his mother paused any longer than this to consider the
	consequences before dropping him off on the doorstep of a
	big city maternity ward?
Did the fee his foster parents were getting from the state for his
	upkeep already seem to him reasonable cause for hating all
	adult society?
Had his own experience to date given him reason to suppose
	himself anything more than a mere burden to that society?
Had he received his First Holy Communion?
Did he comprehend the meaning of sin as proposed in the
	catechism?
Was he the possessor of so much as eight ounces of personal
	property beyond his clothing?
Was he asleep or awake?
Was he really alone in the kitchen?
Was there a slight noise behind him?
Was that his foster father and alleged benefactor standing there
	over him?
Was he being called a thief?
Did he land in a reform school?
Was his head shaved making him look like a boxer with the eyes
	of a mongoloid Rimbaud?
Did he come to stink of urine and institutional disinfectants?
Did he voluntarily plead guilty to unfair charges and suffer
	terrible humiliations on purpose?
Did he join and then desert from the Foreign Legion?
Was he arrested and unjustly accused of stealing a car?
Did he refuse to speak in his own defense?
Was he acquitted as a mental defective?
Did he specialize in the theft of fine books?
Was he a great believer in grammatical laws?
Did he receive an extended sentence?
Did he believe in evil the way mystics believe in God?
Did he lament that all the great grammatical models are dying?

Did he confuse language with his own fate?
Did he ever wonder about the difference between human laws
 and grammatical laws?

Theresa of Avila & The History of Psychology

Up to this point there has been activity effort & movement
All our faculties are still in play
Now however it becomes more than ever necessary
"No longer to think much but to love"
O woman in the mystical desert of Spain
Ride your burro through higher air dimensions
Over the endless bleak austere plateau of Old Castile
Across the basins of the Duero the Tagus & the Guadiana
Landscape ravaged by erosion & of climate severe
As imaginal fields of your El Castillo Interior
And let the bottom line fade & drift away
Preparing yourself for escape into the Great Rapture
The calyxes of the desert blooms have opened only halfway
They have shed only their first perfumes
Through these mauve air waves love moves in the first light of
      day
The being of persons diffused in a stubborn material world
To which you refuse much importance in your psychology
Gray eyes sunken in crystal 500 years rise like dusty pearls
While the pentatonic wind rises out of Africa
The mistral from the Sahara radiates through the spirit world
Theresa of Avila avid in receptivity & translucence
The mistral from the Sahara of powerful love
Confines itself into your intelligent listening flower
Whipped by the hot wind of God as a flag of passion
Made into turbine by the power of your mind
Turned by your water metaphors like bubbling Castilian founts
In the first chamber you articulate your thought out loud
While in the second it becomes inaudible like a flower's
And in the third is clouded by a subtle shade
And in the fourth is replaced by touch
The senses which are still oscillating in chamber five
Are frozen solid in the sixth chamber
As the body grows cold & breathing stops
And then in the seventh chamber a diamond drops
Out of space & grows larger than the world

6. "He Was Born Blind . . ."

Born Blind

He was born blind on the 24th day of May 1904 in Wigan

Imprint of Patriarchs (I)

He was given the name William Booth after the Conqueror by his father James a touring music hall entertainer who had won no little fame locally as the popularizer of the well known Wigan Pier Joke

Mother

His mother Eliza Hoy an Irish Catholic girl produced for James Booth
and for God fourteen children in total of which but seven survived
the first year of existence in gray pinched Wigan

Infancy

Eldest of those not early boxed the blind William was a good natured
but scrawny and rather backward child

First Sight

He finally and dramatically received the gift of sight during a violent coughing fit suffered while being carried in his mother's arms across the Mersey one cold windy morning in the middle of the long rigorous winter of 1905

Student Days

During his first and only year at Notre Dame convent school in Wigan
where he had been placed by his mother he was adjudged deficient
in all subjects particularly Reading and Music

Imprint of Patriarchs (II)

Setting aside his books he followed in the footsteps of his turf-aficionado father developing a precocious interest in horses that was nudged along also by his paternal grandfather a former jockey who now trained horses in Wigan

Withdrawal from Academe

His father purchased a horse and over Eliza's objections withdrew the lad from school at the age of seven and appointed him stable boy

Turf Training

After three years among the barns the boy was shipped across the sea
to Ireland for jockey training

Homecoming

Upon his return from Ireland William hired on with the stable of Lord
Derby as an apprentice rider

Brief Career As Jockey

His hopes were high but he was a washout in the saddle

More Changes

Soon James drifted heavenward forcing a further revision in William's life script

Chance Steps In

In the spring of 1921 still mourning his father and somewhat idly debating the choice of a new career for himself the young man while on a visit to London with his mother happened to stop in at a Victoria Palace Theatre matinee just as a comic on the bill was launching into one of his father's jokes

A Message from Beyond

William interpreted this apparent coincidence as an eerie message from Beyond to the effect that if anyone was going to cash in on the Booth theatrical legacy it ought to be himself

Stage Debut

On the evening of the 21st of April 1921 he made his professional debut as a music hall comedian at Earlestown near Wigan performing under his mother's surname Hoy a small mercy for which his father probably would have been grateful

First Reviews

Reviews were indifferent at best

Early Struggles

For three years he struggled along on sheer nerve playing to negligible crowds in cheap houses and hanging on mainly because he couldn't think of anything better to do with himself

Encounter With Clog Dancer (I)

Then one night in a boarding house on the circuit he encountered a smiling moon faced twenty year old clog dancer from Accrington named Beryl Ingham

Life Script Revision

Aboard the galactic program ship *Atlantis* William's Booth/Hoy script
was immediately rerun with erasures and inserts

Happy Event

On Friday the 13th day of September 1924 Beryl became William's wife and within a few weeks also his business manager booking agent hairstylist clothes designer publicist and song and dance coach

Starting Over

To begin William's remaking from the ground up Beryl suggested they find him a new name something to distinguish him from other stand-up comics by playing up rather than attempting to conceal the appearance of gawkish witlessness which was his most noticeable personal trait

A New Name

"That gormless lad from Lancashire" as he would soon become known selected for himself the name George Formby which his father had once pointed out with delight on the side of a railway carriage and which exactly suited the bland classless look Beryl now had in mind for him

A Shtick

Beryl equipped him with a ukelele and taught him to strum three chords on it and croon along while at the same time overtly employing it as a comical phallic surrogate

Imagemaking

William/George was dressed up in evening clothes neutrally perfect down to the ruler-sharp part bisecting hair which slickly clasped his skull thanks to last minute palmfuls of Brylcreem slapped on in his dressing room by Beryl

A Star Is Born

Everything worked out exactly as programmed in Script Revision the
knowing wink the wicky wacky grin the suggestive little uke stroking
out the last ounce of implication in Auntie Maggie's Remedy Old
Grandad's Flannelette Nightshirt My Little Stick of Blackpool Rock

Sex Equals Money

Of all his biggest hit songs only Leaning On A Lamppost was
completely free of sexual innuendo because as Beryl had carefully
planned it George Formby was good clean fun *but* also a bit of the other

George's Little Secret

What people all over Britain found so attractive about George Form-by was his appearance of tilting against social codes of repression without knowing it while delivering such slightly off-color lyrics as those of his 1937 hit When I'm Cleaning Windows

What the Window Cleaner Saw

Pyjamas lying side by side Ladies nighties I have spied I've often seen what went inside When I'm Cleaning Windows

Influence of the Crown

The Royal Family became great George Formby admirers and pulled strings to see to it that whenever he performed at Windsor Castle or at Marlborough his naughty songs would be done in the uncensored versions

Trouble With Dominant Organ of Culture

Royal sanction however was not enough to get George's songs past
the BBC which suppressed Cleaning Windows even in elaborately
sanitized recorded versions

Beryl Strikes Back

The ensuing censorship controversy climaxed with a BBC announcer's arch comment that George Formby's windows still weren't clean enough causing Beryl to erupt in an explosion of angry phonecalls to important ministers she knew socially and as a result a unique editorial apology was broadcast just before the nine o'clock news

Silver Screen

Going into movies on Beryl's gentle but firm insistence in 1934 George became an instant smash and was soon starring opposite such stunning young women as Phyllis Calvert Pat Kirkwood Florence Desmond and Googie Withers though Beryl brooked no flirting on the set

Spartan Stardom

George accustomed himself to ignoring female fans around the studio and proceeding directly from soundstage to dressing room for spare meals prepared on a portable cookstove by Beryl

His Allowance

Beryl restricted the naturally adventuresome comedian to an allowance of five shillings a day ferreting the remainder of his earnings in the bank

Speed and Stunts

Even his dangerous love of boiling engines and speed which inspired him to race automobiles motor bikes anything with four or two wheels and in 1939 to become the first man to circumnavigate the Brooklands track at over one hundred miles per hour was eventually harnessed to the efficient Formby career dynamo as he now became his own stunt man in movies mounting a race horse again for the first time in several decades in Come On George 1940

Imprint of Patriarchs (III)

With Let George Do It 1941 the George Formby fame beacon turned
eastward as the mature entertainer (no doubt with his own father in
mind) played an old vaudevillian singing and dancing his way blithe-
ly past agents of the Third Reich

Let George Do It

was a light spy spoof whistling its way through the darkness of the Anschluss so popular with English sailors and their Russian girlfriends at the British navy base in Murmansk a dubbed version titled Dinky Do was turned out by the Soviet culture ministry and played to full houses in Moscow for a solid year at the end of which George Formby officially ranked beneath only Stalin and a few generals as the most popular man in the USSR

The War

George went out touring the troops for Monty in a long exhausting junket through the Middle East and North Africa with Gracie Fields

In the Desert

In the middle of the desert away from Beryl and all things familiar George found himself completely happy and thought nothing of crawling down into a slit trench to extend a cheery hello to one of his military fans

Looking for the Rank and File

Ever the ordinary man's friend he went out of his way to express his
displeasure with the way army big shots and their wives were taking
all the best seats at his shows and finally held up a show outside
Tobruk to ask for a telescope so that he could see the rank and file

Power of Comedy

George's joke caused a disorderly demonstration to break out among overstressed troops at the rear of the packed tent

Effects of Comedy

News of the disturbance traveled back to Montgomery and beyond
and as a consequence when the shooting was over George did not
receive the knighthood he secretly coveted

Beryl Ponders

When the shooting stopped Beryl saw a changed script on the wall

Consequence of War

The war had brought George a broad new mixed class audience that
included ex-officers who were once again attending West End plays

Beryl's Decision

Beryl decided it was time for George to re-enter the theatre this time by the front door

The Stage

His first West End hit was Zip Goes A Million 1951

Followup Movie Deal

Beryl soon clinched a followup movie deal in six figures locking George into the full nelson of a ninety percent income tax bracket forever

Wheels of Fortune

Beryl had long since zipped away a small fortune in cash so that each
of them could now afford a new car every year usually a Bentley or
a Jag for George but for Beryl always a Rolls

800 Wheels

The Formbys' 200th car was a Rolls-Royce for Beryl priced at six thousand two hundred and fifty pounds

Crisis on the Cruiser

Soon afterwards as they were enjoying a break from shooting the film version of Zip Goes A Million George suffered a coronary thrombosis at their luxury cruiser on the Norfolk Broads

Once Again Beyond Names

A medical team led by the King's physician fought to save his life as he lay sedated and partially conscious trying to recall his name and from the East End to Perth to Vancouver anxious fans implored Come On George to remind him

Medical Opinions

After the crisis Queen Mary begged him to cut back on his heavy
schedule for the sake of the millions who loved him and his doctors'
advice ran along the same lines

Beryl's Advice

Beryl however urged him to finish up the picture back in London and
so he did

Fate Pressing

Beryl continued to represent fate pressing him on with gentle karmic force at his side in a million smiling publicity photographs yet it was also now true that in private they quarreled terribly like twin beings each of whom will be released from hell only by the other's extinction

Slide Area

Beryl's second drink of the afternoon now too often spilled over an edge into nights that encapsulated the pain of several very nasty animal eternities throughout which she was constantly ill and drinking heavily to ease the line noise coming in over Radio Atlantis

Drifting Spindle

She began to drift and given just that much slack George started to ride out away into himself so that on the shooting set and during rehearsals those around him supposed he was worrying about his heart when he lapsed into a strange vacant look like a man imagining the deep future

Dimming

The Formby sparkle had begun to dim down into an intermittent
twinkle as in the longer and longer intervals between jobs he spent
extended periods off breeding horses at his mansion near Dublin

Late Release

As Beryl gradually faded out of the picture upstairs like a stain slowly receding George was at last able to get his hands on his own money
and take off after one final dream

Imprint of the Patriarchs (IV)

He bought the estate of the celebrated tenor Josef Locke at Fairhaven near Blackpool and embarked on a surprising return to the common stage of his origins appearing unexpectedly at local summer shows variety acts and pantomimes a sad strumming shadow of himself as in the mothy phantom lit wings old James Booth hid his face in his hands

Beryl Beamed In

At this point the frail diminishing signal of the fatecast that had held
George Formby on course for 36 years gave out completely or so it
was feared by many in his adoring public as on Christmas morning
1960 Beryl was beamed home for good

Public Opinion

At the difficult age of 56 and with a failing ticker George was left alone and assumed by his devoted legions to be sunk in an eternal gormless desolation

A Surprise

Instead he shocked everyone by announcing not long after seeing Beryl off into the dark ground that he was about to marry a bright and healthy young Lancashire schoolteacher named Pat

Meeting the Press

Amid the national furor of protest that followed he held a dramatic press conference at which he expressed his hope that his fans would not begrudge him this one moment of happiness and his intention to proceed with plans for an April wedding whether anybody liked it or not

Too Much for Him

On the sixth day of March 1961 Pat showed him the diamond wedding ring she had just bought and George produced one last feeble
gormless grin then with a sigh of weariness descended directly to the
shades

Encounter With Clog Dancer (II)

His body was placed in his father's grave and once again he could see nothing but after a while there started up a barely audible music not unlike the sound of clogs lightly tapping on the sides of the box

Printed February 1990 in Santa Barbara & Ann
Arbor for the Black Sparrow Press by Graham
Mackintosh & Edwards Brothers Inc. Text set in
Trump by Words Worth. Design by Barbara Martin.
This edition is published in paper wrappers;
there are 250 hardcover trade copies;
150 hardcover copies have been numbered
& signed by the author; & 26 lettered copies have
been handbound in boards by Earle Gray, each with
an original drawing by Tom Clark.

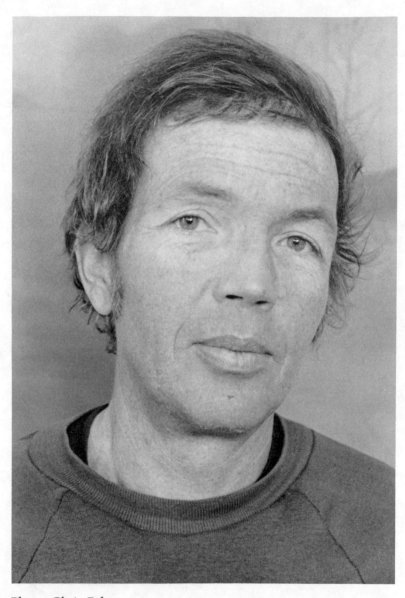

Photo: Chris Felver

Tom Clark's books include many volumes of poetry, from *Air* (1970) and *Stones* (1970) to four volumes of selected poems from Black Sparrow, *When Things Get Tough on Easy Street* (1978), *Paradise Resisted* (1984), *Disordered Ideas* (1987), and *Fractured Karma* (1990). He is also the author of novels (*Who Is Sylvia?, The Exile of Céline*), literary essays (*The Poetry Beat: Reviewing the Eighties*), and biographies (*The World of Damon Runyon, Jack Kerouac, Late Returns: A Memoir of Ted Berrigan*). He is currently at work on a life of the American poet Charles Olson.